BUSINESS TO GO

simple ideas to takeaway

Andrew B Morris

Matador
9 Priory Business Park
Wistow Road
Kibworth
Leics LE8 0RX
Tel: 0116 279 2299
www.troubador.co.uk/matador

ISBN: 9781780882291

Illustration and Design by Otto
www.ottographic.co.uk

Matador is an imprint of Troubador Publishing Ltd

FSC
www.fsc.org

MIX
Paper from
responsible sources
FSC® C013056

Printed and bound in Great Britain by
TJ International Ltd, Padstow, Cornwall

dedicated to the memory of

Max Miller

who left us wanting more

"To laugh is to risk being the fool. To weep is to risk appearing sentimental. To reach out for another is to risk involvement. To show feelings is to risk exposing your true self.

To place your ideas, your dreams, before the crowd is to risk their loss. To love is to risk not being loved in return. To live is to risk dying. To hope is to risk despair. To try is to risk failure.

But risk must be taken because the greatest hazard in life is to risk nothing. Those who risk nothing, do nothing, have nothing and are nothing. They may avoid suffering and sorrow but they cannot learn, feel, change, grow, love or truly live. Chained by their certitude's they are slaves.

They have forfeited their freedom.

Only a person who risks is truly free."

Leo F. Buscaglia

GOING FASTER

I have always been fascinated by business and by people and wondered why it is that some make it and some don't. I am convinced that if we are able to apply some basic principles, in a disciplined way, our businesses will grow, but if we over complicate matters we will remain commentators rather than participants.

Having spent many years running organisations, some quite large and some very small, I am now in a support role trying to help leaders be more impactful whilst leading a balanced life. Grow the leader and they will transform the business.

Today's head-spinningly fast pace demands that to grow we have to learn fast too. I felt that if there was a way to learn on the go, a way to land the learning in the moment, and put it into practice there and then, this could be very useful.

So that is what BUSINESS TO GO sets out to achieve.

Dip in according to what you need to know right now and I hope you find the ideas and thinking simple to takeaway, adapt to your situation, and apply.

If we keep it simple and concise, use our common sense and instinct, laced with a healthy portion of passion, we should stop talking and start doing.

Contents

YOU CAN JUDGE A BOOK BY ITS COVER — 8
OUR MOST UNDER-USED WORDS — 11
TRANSPARENCY WORKS BEST — 12
MAKE 'EM LAUGH! — 15
VALUES – THE POST-IT WAY — 16
DEAD DAD SYNDROME — 18
GOOD & BAD STRESS — 20
180 DAYS — 22
TWO TRIBES — 24
CELEBRATE OUR HISTORY — 25
THE SLEEP-OVER TEST — 26
VOTE FOR ME — 28
LITTLE THINGS — 30
THE HOMELY OFFICE — 32
HOW ARE YOU FEELING? — 34
UNFORCED ERRORS — 36
WATCH OUT THERE'S AN NED ABOUT — 38
POLISH YOUR SWORD — 40
THE CEO JOB SPEC — 42
BRING YOURSELF TO WORK — 44
THE FOLLOW SPOT — 46
BEING SIMPLE — 48
KEEP IT SHORT — 50
PITCH PERFECT — 52

PROFIT SHOULD BE SEEN AND NOT HEARD 54
BEING FAMOUS 56
IDEAS, PEOPLE & CASH 58
THE TOP LINE 60
WRITE IT RIGHT 62
THE BURNING PLATFORM 64
A FEW GREAT PEOPLE 66
WHAT ARE WE DOING RIGHT? 68
DON'T LET THE DETAIL DESTROY THE DEAL 70
SHUT UP 72
MAKING A CRISIS LESS OF A DRAMA 74
PREP OR IMPROV 76
START-UPS 78
STOP DOING, START THINKING 80
A GOAL SETTING PROCESS 82
CORPORATE HEALTH CHECK 84
ENCORE ANXIETY 86
RISKY BUSINESS 88
REBEL WITH A CAUSE 90
SELL TOO EARLY 91
HIGH TIME FOR A 'CSO' 92

WE CAN JUDGE A BOOK BY ITS COVER

The need to make a positive first impression – **the handshake moment** – is critical in attracting people.

Contrary to popular myth, we **can** make an accurate assessment within the first moments of meeting someone for the first time. According to recent research, within the first 7 seconds we can make a balanced judgement on 11 key characteristics, shown on the opposite page.

And, amazingly, our assessment will be **80% accurate.**

This is not necessarily about superficial stuff, like grooming and dress sense, but more about our primeval instincts, where 'sniffing' someone told us whether they were friend or foe.

So, if a first instinct suggests they are untrustworthy, keep a wide berth. But if intuition suggests they are credible and successful, keep talking,

Now consider what others see in you at that handshake moment.

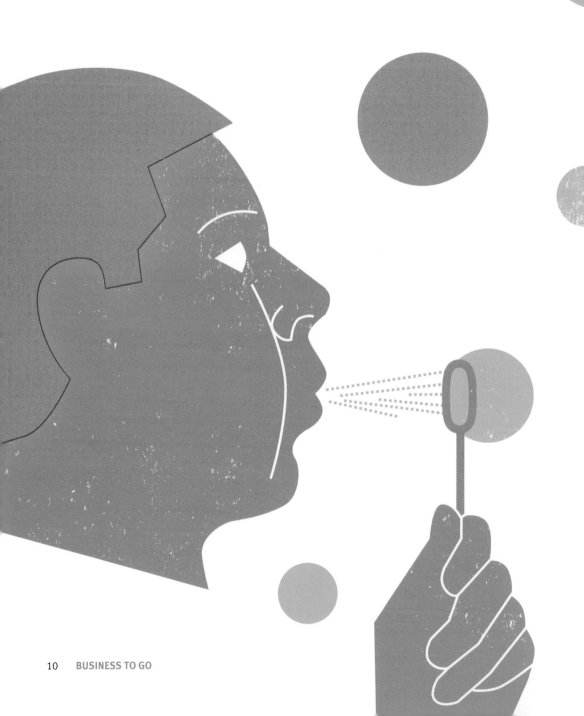

OUR MOST UNDER-USED WORDS

Why do so many leaders ignore common courtesy, make out they know all the answers, rarely apologise or acknowledge a job well done?

Saying **'Thanks'** cost nothing but means a lot.

Saying **'Well done'** means more than a bonus.

Saying **'Sorry'** kills contempt.

And saying 'I don't know..but will find out' wins us far more respect than bull-shitting.

Be Straight

Be Honest

Be Human

We all know when you're not.

If we screw up, say so.

If we offend a colleague, don't let it fester.

If they've done well, tell them.

And if we don't know the answer, or understand the question, show strength by saying so.

TRANSPARENCY WORKS BEST

Bosses regularly reflect on how much information they should share with their people. Too much and they'll get confused. Too little and they're left in the dark. Results that are too good might encourage salary increases. Results that are too bad may create insecurity.

How do we find the right balance?

The jungle drum ensures our people know much more than we realise and are far smarter than we may recognise. If our work-force are constantly kept in the picture, they stay engaged and become our best PRs, spreading accurate and positive stuff about us.

Ignorance breeds mistrust
Information promotes understanding

If we present our facts and figures in a concise and consistent way, our people become accustomed to the statistics, easily comparing our progress month by month. Get bad news out fast and hold onto good news until it's signed and sealed.

'Town Hall' gatherings, presented in a fun and creative way by our teams, rather than management, are really effective ways to communicate and maintain engagement. And..

..send emails to your people from your home on Sunday afternoons when they're most receptive and getting into 'back to work' mode.

'Only one man in a thousand is a leader of men.

The other 999 is a follower of women.'

MAKE 'EM LAUGH

The use of humour in the business environment is often misunderstood. The comedian can be seen as unreliable, using jokes and wit as a defence mechanism.

Used in the right way, making someone smile, or better still, laugh out loud, is a great reliever of tension, especially when times are tough. Laughter releases endorphins which naturally induce that wonderful feel-good feeling.

We might try to use wit and humour to create a special character which makes us distinctive. Especially if we're in one of those boring sectors (we know who we are) that lack a distinctive quality.

The word 'fun' often appears within a set of corporate values.

Perhaps 'funny' would be better.

A market trader is lecturing his grandson on the importance of ethics in business. "So, yesterday this bloke walks in and buys a 20 quid shirt. He pays cash, but, as he's walking out, I notice he's given me two twenty pound notes stuck together. Now" the trader says, radiating wisdom "This is where ethics comes in. I have to ask myself this question: Do I tell my partner?"

VALUES – THE POST-IT WAY

Walk into most businesses and you'll see a set of slick values stuck on a wall. Few notice them, most can't recall their origin.

Consultants charge fortunes to run endless workshops that are intended to arrive at a set of authentic values that capture an organisation's DNA.

Don't bother - this exercise can be done in an evening.

Step 1   Assemble the team in a relaxing environment, ideally after work, possibly with a few drinks.

Step 2   Put up 3 boards, with a header on one saying **WE ARE (in green):** another saying **WE NEVER (in red):** and another saying **WE WANT TO (in blue):** Give out post-it notes, in each of these colours, to all present.

Step 3   Explain that **WE ARE:** describes our current values, **WE NEVER:** describes what we never want to be, and **WE WANT TO:** describes what we'd like to be. Each member of the top team then writes a statement (best prepared earlier) on a post-it and sticks it on the relevant board. The rest of the team are then invited to do the same and so the process begins. This is likely to take a few hours as people are only encouraged to submit their post-its when they feel ready.

Step 4   We now have a bunch of value statements that have come directly and honestly from the hearts of our people. Group them into themes, remove duplications, photograph and frame the results.

These authentic values, created inclusively, will last the test of time.

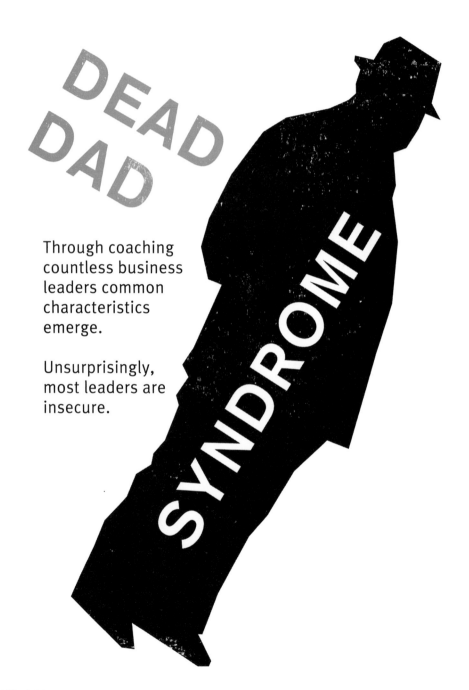

DEAD DAD SYNDROME

Through coaching countless business leaders common characteristics emerge.

Unsurprisingly, most leaders are insecure.

More interestingly, many male leaders are trying to prove, or disprove, something to their Dad.

Perhaps we feel our Dad was a bit of a loser, and we're desperate not to repeat this with our own life. Or our Dad was a great success, and we feel lost in his shadow. Or, he just never gave us enough time or respect or praise.

These feelings lead to a compelling drive to succeed.

On the trading floors of the City, where only peak performance, every day, is acceptable, they recognise Dead Dad Syndrome and apply it. Many of the best male traders have lost their Dads and this is revealed at the interview stage, and seen as positive. These guys tend to be the most focused, the most intense, and the most successful.

If your Dad is still around, I hope he gives you the praise and support you need, both as a parent and as a mentor. And if he's passed on, you have fond memories of your relationship.

And, if you have a son, don't forget how much he craves your time, your love and your appreciation.

GOOD STRESS AND BAD STRESS

Just like we have good and bad cholesterol, so we have good and bad stress.

will motivate, give us supreme confidence, stimulate creative thinking and enhance our decision making.

Bad stress will impact our sleep, distort our perspective and judgement, and, if left unchecked for too long, even lead to burn-out.

So, how do we encourage good stress within ourselves? By ensuring that...

▶   We feel in control of the situation at all times
▶   We are driving our agenda
▶   We are doing what we want to be doing

What's really important to ME – instead of what someone, or something, is doing to me.

Being in this zone is sublime and is when we do our best work. It takes great discipline and self-awareness, as well as the ability to say 'NO.' When we feel ourselves slipping into bad stress, when events start to take hold, stop, take a breath, and re-establish control.

Good stress brings with it boundless energy and is an indicator that we're in the driving seat.

drains energy and says we're just a passenger being taken where we don't want to go.

180 DAYS

Recruiting new talent is fundamental to growth and needs to be undertaken in a measured manner as a part of a well thought through process, evaluating skills, experience, ambition, culture and values. This is all highly objective because, at this stage, there is no emotional attachment to the candidate or the decision to appoint them.

When we finally decide who gets the job we own the responsibility of being proved right, making the right call on this hire. This obsession with being right can sometimes blind our objectivity during that all important probationary period.

We are often guilty of hanging on to new people for far longer than we should, because we're so keen to see them succeed, and our decision to hire them, vindicated. The cost and time to replace them, the acceptance we made a mistake, all weigh heavily.

After 12 months they are still with us, still not doing what we pay them for.

At 18 months, bowing to pressure from our colleagues, we finally let them go.

The cost of hiring the wrong people is impossible to calculate but is HUGE. We take their failure to succeed very personally. We see it as a reflection on us.

WAKE UP!
180 days is enough time to know if they're right.

We come
across
two tribes
of people
in the
business
world.
The Do-ers...
who do what they
say, or agreed to do.
The Talk-ers... who do not.

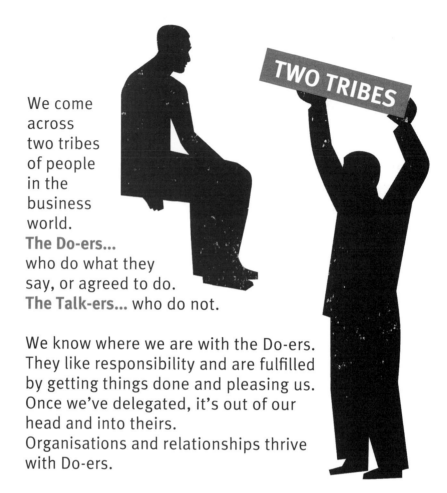

We know where we are with the Do-ers.
They like responsibility and are fulfilled
by getting things done and pleasing us.
Once we've delegated, it's out of our
head and into theirs.
Organisations and relationships thrive
with Do-ers.

Talk-ers say, with sincerity, 'leave it
with me' but quickly forget what we left.
They pretend to make notes.
They make excuses for letting us down, and ask for
deadlines to be extended, more than once.
In short, they over promise and don't deliver.
Organisations and relationships can be destroyed by
the Talk-ers.

Which tribe would you prefer to belong to?

CELEBRATE OUR HISTORY

When we stay at an old country house hotel, or eat at a long established restaurant or pub, we often find ourselves fascinated by reading the brochure or the menu. 'An old hunting lodge frequented by Henry VIII' catches your attention and makes you feel special.

 A sense of place. The history matters to us.

Our business life story should illuminate our workplace and our marketing. Company social events, exhibitions and conferences, press coverage, charitable activities – all expressing...

'We have a history and we're proud of it.'

Don't be shy about displaying 'thank you' letters from customers, awards or even letters from staff saying how great it is to work here.

Showing our history, both internally and externally, gives us added credibility, makes us even more interesting, and creates a context in which we operate today. It sets us apart from all those start-ups who have no history to tell.

If you have a history – flaunt it!

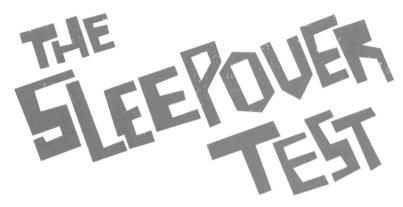

THE SLEEPOVER TEST

We all recognise how important it is to establish whether a potential new recruit will fit our values and culture. Their experience and skills look fine, but will they feel at home with our style?

One way to quickly work out whether they will be a good fit is the Sleep-Over Test.

Would we invite this person, metaphorically, to our home to sleep-over?

If the thought of them staying with us for a night fills us with horror, they're unlikely to be a good fit.

If we can see ourselves having a pleasant evening, feeling relaxed with them in our home and with our family, then they're likely to be a fine fit.

And whilst the idea of a sleep-over is extreme, actually inviting them home for a meal, so they can get a real sense of who you are, and they can reflect on whether you are the right fit for them.

If you want to know the dog – sleep in his kennel.

If we had
only had
3 years to
make a real
difference,
would we be
inclined to
move that
much faster
and more
decisively?

VOTE FOR ME

Few leaders of a corporate organisation have ever been elected to office by a popular vote of all stakeholders.

So what!?

Well, any leader who loses the support of their followers has lost their mandate to lead. Staying connected with our followers, turning them into collaborators, is how we continue to lead effectively.

Would we keep our job if the decision was made by a democratic vote of our staff, shareholders, suppliers and customers?

Whilst democracy is far from perfect, it's still the best way to test whether our performance is supported by those who we count on to deliver the results.

Leaders who outstay their welcome tend to get overthrown in a pretty unpleasant manner, losing their dignity and reputation in the process.

Although politicians have many failings, the fact that they hold power for a limited period presses them to avoid wasting time and energetically drive change.

LITTLE THINGS

People rarely work for financial gain as their top priority. They might tell us that when negotiating their pay, but they won't stay if they don't like their colleagues, our culture, environment, or the way they are treated.

In other words, how their work makes them feel.

We can make our people feel very good with very little cost, and just a little thought...

► A handwritten note of appreciation or anniversary - on a card that is relevant
► Ice creams or lollies when the weather is really hot
► Praise in the moment – in front of colleagues (if this won't embarrass) or privately if this means more
► Time with us – a coffee, chat or meal
► A turkey at Christmas – means so much coming from the boss
► A recommendation if they have a health problem..
..paying for a consultant if we can afford it..
..and a get well card..
..and a hospital visit if we know them well enough

► Remembering the names of loved ones and asking how they're doing
► Suggesting time off if they deserve it or need it – not waiting to be asked..
► Perhaps suggesting what they might do to recharge

And so on....

Years later, when we reconnect with people who have moved on, the first thing they will fondly recall when they see us is not the size of their bonus, but all the little things we did which really touched them and showed we cared.

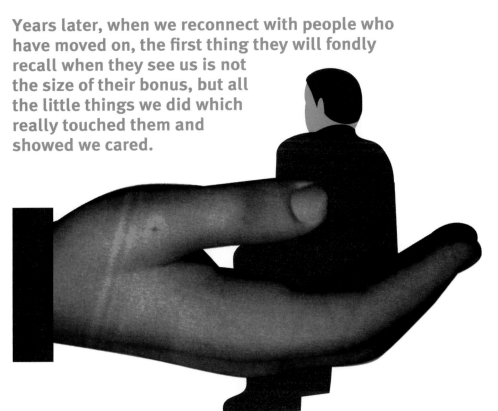

A HOMELY OFFICE

My wife once said to me at a b&b somewhere in Suffolk: "Why are we staying at a hotel that's less comfortable than my home?" She had a point and after that I tried harder.

We spend over half our lives in the workplace and notice how much more productive we are when we are comfortable and relaxed.

 **So why do so many employers have such a mean attitude to the place that creates the cash for them to finance their lifestyle?**

It's not indulgent to have air-conditioning now our climate is milder and more humid. Heat makes you lethargic, smelly and dehydrated – not great for productivity or image.

Comfortable, ergonomic chairs with proper lumber support, set at the right height for our keyboard, will avoid back and circulation problems and R.S.I. And a possible claim.

And a pleasant environment, with a splash of colour, some decent graphics, photos or pictures on the walls, perhaps with the odd plant, all makes it a more human, and homely, place to be.

An army marches on its stomach, so, if we can't provide kitchen facilities, make available a list of good local places to eat and drink. It's healthy to take a break from our desk during the day and will help recharge us for the afternoon.

The more homely our place of work, the more time our people will productively spend there.

HOW ARE YOU FEELING?

Today's executives, particularly blokes, find it difficult to talk about their feelings, especially at work. Asked how we're feeling, we'll be surprised and off guard, and uncomfortably respond with a mumble of "..fine" "..ok" or "..good."

Our emotions take dominance in our decision taking over our rational brain. Once we've collated all the data and research, calculated the budget and prepared the plan, our final decision to proceed or delay will be based upon one key emotion:

c   o   n   f   i   d   e   n   c   e

So it's surprising that we don't get into the habit of asking how we're feeling rather more often. Here's a powerful way to check morale and mood. At the start of a meeting, ask everyone to say how they are feeling, and why, banning the words "Fine, OK, or Good."

Here's an example:

"I'm feeling **concerned** because we're behind budget for the third month in a row."
"I'm feeling **excited** because our new supplier has improved our margin by 7%."
"I'm feeling **frustrated** because it's taking too long to introduce the new sales software across the company."

This process will reveal what's really going on under the surface and show whether there is a confidence problem that needs confronting. We focus on tasks and actions, not what's behind them.

How we are being can be as important as what we are doing.
We are human beings not human doings.

UNFORCED ERRORS

Watching tennis demonstrates there's one statistic that makes the critical difference between winning and losing. Forget 'First Serve Percentage' or 'Outright Winners', it's the 'Number of Unforced Errors' that really matters to the result.

This statistic shows
consistency
and that is how we win.

In sport.

In business.

Some entrepreneurs will succeed through one good idea – the outright winner – or being aggressive and committed – the first serve percentage – but most will get there by minimising mistakes, or unforced errors.

When we launch something entirely new, we can't avoid making many mistakes in our first year.
Ever noticed how much easier the second year feels, and how much quicker it all takes? With experience our unforced errors are massively reduced.

REDUCING UNFORCED ERRORS

1. Sleep on it. Never make a big decision at the end of a working day, when we're tired and our perspective is poor. It will look very different in the morning.

2. Find a Man that Can. Someone who has been there and done it before – an industry expert.

3. Get a Mentor. Someone who has proven commercial experience who challenges our thinking and judgement and help us make the right decisions.

'Whatever failures I have known, whatever errors I have committed, whatever follies I have witnessed, have been the consequences of action without thought.'

WATCH OUT THERE'S AN NED ABOUT

Do we get real value from our Non-Executive Directors or are they simply there to appease our shareholders and provide corporate governance? I believe the majority meet this description.

Too many NEDs turn up for board meetings, having not read the papers thoroughly, or at all, and then pretend to understand what is going on, making the odd comment to justify their fee. Recognise this?

This poor behaviour is not their fault, it's ours.

▶ Did we agree a specific role, and outputs, in the same way we would for an executive director?
▶ Did we decide what skill was lacking around the board table?
▶ Did we check their portfolio to establish how much time and thought they can devote to us?
▶ Did we set down a method by which their contribution can be regularly and objectively evaluated?
▶ Did we make it clear to whom they should report?
▶ Did we induct them properly so that they had a good understanding of our business?
▶ Did we ask them to buy shares to demonstrate their commitment?
▶ Did we consider whether we needed an NED in the first place?

It may be more effective to appoint an Advisor rather than an NED, as they can be more direct with their input, standing outside board room politics.

POLISH YOUR SWORD

Previous perceived wisdom for training leaders would involve developing a number of core skills: communication, listening, decision taking, stress management, vision, strategy, and so on. But can you be great at all of them and is that really necessary?

10% of us are born leaders, 10% could never lead anything and 80% can develop leadership skills with the right training and approach. But what kind of approach?

SWORD & SHIELD

Our Sword keeps us on the offensive, thrusting forward, by using our natural talent. Keep our Sword constantly polished, refining our techniques to even greater effect, remembering the power and strength it can wield.

Our Shield defends us against those demons that make us feel weak and vulnerable. The stuff that doesn't come naturally. Be conscious of these but don't bother trying to fix them. (You will spend a lifetime trying to shape a shield into a sword).

Work out how
best to defend.
If we're bad with
numbers or detail,
let someone who
is better do this
for us. If we're
not good on
our feet giving
speeches or
presentations,
don't beat
ourselves up,
step aside
and find
someone who
can.

Focus on what
you're naturally
good at .. and
become brilliant
at it.

Defend or delegate what
you're hopeless at .. and don't
fret about it.

THE CEO JOB SPEC

Every Chief Executive or MD brings their unique talent and style to the organisation they lead. Some are creative, some financial doctors, some industry gurus, some technical geniuses, some great communicators, some just bring boundless energy and enthusiasm.

Commentators have endlessly debated the critical ingredients that, above and beyond our day job, a CEO MUST bring to the organisation.

The keys to unlock eternal health, wealth and growth.

Here now are my BIG THREE:

1.   **VISION – where we are going..**

The CEO sets out the organisation's deeply desired future and clearly communicates this to all who will help get us there. Also, articulating the 'magic dust' which sets us apart.

2.   **TALENT – who's going to get us there?**

The CEO is the chief talent scout, constantly on the lookout for great new people who will take us to the promised land of our Vision. Then ensuring this new

talent is welcomed into the organisation, and nurtured, given the wings to fly to great heights.

3. **CULTURE – how we act when we're at our best**

The CEO is the custodian of corporate culture, outlawing what does not fit, and nourishing what does, recruiting against these values. THE role model, constantly vigilant of breaches and lapses, especially when we're under great pressure.

BRING YOURSELF TO WORK

Fact: We spend a huge proportion of our lives at work.

Fact: We tend to wear a mask at work and don't show enough of our true selves.

Fact: Distorting who we are, bending ourselves out of shape each working day, is extremely tiring and stressful.

Fact: People can spot when we are not being authentic and this generates mistrust and unsettles relationships.

Fact: Constant stress leads to poor performance and bad physical and mental health.

Question: So, is it ok to show my vulnerability and insecurity at work?

Answer: Absolutely. This displays enormous self-confidence.

Question: I've been wearing the corporate mask so long, how will I know when I'm really being myself?

Answer:

You'll feel comfortable in your own skin.
Your shoulders will relax.
Your breathing will slow.
You will feel calmer.
Your clarity and energy will increase.
Your voice will be the same outside and inside work.
People will like and respect you more.

Ask them.

THE FOLLOW SPOT

As a Leader, everyone is watching us, all of the time.

Like a spotlight following our every move, illuminating every action and reaction.

When we disengage at a meeting, and our mind wanders off to more pressing matters, don't think everyone present doesn't notice. We're saying 'This isn't important to me.'

Just like our computers we can ..

| Hibernate | Restart | Sleep | Shutdown |

many times during the working day.

If we're usually pretty upbeat, if our mood is down a notch or two, we're sending out a signal that says 'I'm concerned.' We may just be preoccupied but this unsettles our team.

As an authority figure in our organisation we need to be constantly conscious of our

State and Presence

Any inconsistency will be immediately spotted, raising concern.

Like an actor on stage, our performance is constantly being scrutinised.

The follow spot is relentless.

BEING SIMPLE

The biggest brains don't necessarily make the best business people.

Business is mostly about common sense and those blessed with a high IQ have a tendency to over complicate and over analyse. (A high EQ will get you further). The preoccupation with academic qualifications are impressive on the CV but are not a guarantee we'll make it in the commercial world.

Keeping it simple is central to running a successful enterprise.

Our business model to our budget to our assets to our product range.

If we're unable to retain these fundamentals in our head, our business has become too complicated, or too big. (Or our memory is going!)

Our accountants insist on reams of spread-sheets and analysis, using their big brains to over inform and clutter our thinking.

Our lawyers send us war and peace on that deal, pages upon pages of pointless points, designed to protect them against a claim.

> If key information can't be contained on a single A4 page, reject it. We have more than enough to read and think about every day.

KEEP IT SHORT

The most complex issues can be communicated in just a few short words.

And should be.

The preamble can become like a trailer to a film. So long and detailed that we lose the will to see the film itself.

No-one is interested in the great fight to win the deal. We're only interested in the result and the impact it will have.

The ability to present information in a concise manner is a gift to the listener.

Life's too short – get to the point.

Less is more.

Save being a raconteur to celebrities on chat shows or boozy dinners.

(Sorry I took so long to make this point)

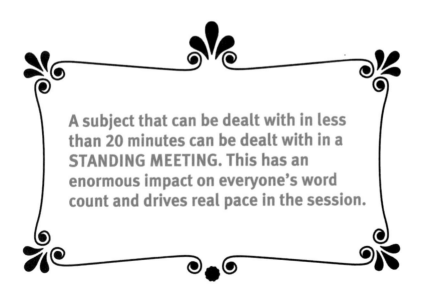

A subject that can be dealt with in less than 20 minutes can be dealt with in a STANDING MEETING. This has an enormous impact on everyone's word count and drives real pace in the session.

PITCH PERFECT

Whether we are presenting our company to a potential partner, bank, customer or whoever, getting it right makes the difference between winning and losing.
This can be a costly and time consuming exercise, and being match fit by rehearsing properly is what it is all about.

PREPARATION

▶ Who's On Our Team? Agree roles and a Team Leader.

▶ Know Their Team. Who is the ultimate decision maker?

▶ Is The Brief And Criteria For Selection Clear? If not, try to renegotiate. If they resist, consider withdrawing.

▶ Where, When & How Long? Get the logistics right.

▶ Documentation, Material & Format. What information will we leave behind?

▶ Who Else Is Pitching? Know the enemy. What's the running order?

- Dress Code. Respect theirs but stay true to our style and image.

FIRST IMPRESSIONS
- Seating Plan. Try to integrate both teams avoiding them and us.
- Introductions. Be clear on who does what and who says what.
- Getting Settled. Some small talk, if possible, before you begin.

THE PRESENTATION
- Open With Impact. A statement, an image, a question.
- The Observer & Scribe. One of our team to watch, listen and note.
- Stick To The Brief. Don't deviate unless they do.
- Hand-Out Now Or Later? At the close works best.
- Q&A + Comment. Maximise engagement and interaction.
- Entertain. Be creative and anything but boring.
- Close Strongly. Possibly re-stating your opening.
- Feedback. It's ok to ask for their reaction and impressions.
- Next Steps. Who should speak to whom and by when? Is any further information required?
- Note The 'Goodbye' This can be the most revealing moment of all.

PROFIT SHOULD BE SEEN ...

Monthly profit & loss, balance sheet and especially cash flow are obviously essential tools for monitoring the progress of our business.

But we may be in danger of allowing ourselves to become overly obsessed with the numbers.

When we're trying to lose weight getting on the scales each day is pretty pointless. If we watch our calories, and step up the exercise, we'll lose those pounds, so jumping on the scales becomes academic. The scales keep count but, aside from encouragement, don't have any direct impact on the goal.

This is also true of the numbers.

If we're on top of the things that really matter in our company, constantly referring to our financial reports can be counter-productive.

Our best results are achieved when we know we're doing our best work, and this will automatically flow to the bottom line.

It's not safe to keep looking at the instruments on the dashboard on our car. Look at the road ahead and be aware of what's around us.

. . AND NOT HEARD

The profit we make is simply a measure of the quality of our output in and around the company. Just like the scales and the dashboard, they don't help us get there any quicker, and can be a disarming distraction.

Any business without a genuine differentiation ends up being a commodity, subordinated to selling on price alone. This is a sad and lonely place to be and is usually populated by miserable faces.

Setting ourselves apart from the competition, being special, is rewarding and exhilarating, and allows us to command a premium price.

Going one step further elevates us to ...being famous!

ry business has the capacity to be famous for
ething.

Famous Product – a tough call but great if we can
get there.
Famous Service – companies that never say 'no'
Famous Boss – for the person who loves celebrity
Famously Innovative – where the culture is a
creative one
Famous to Work For – for companies who love their
staff
Famously Fast – at customer response and delivery

rching for our piece of fame is fun and
ivational, leading us to opportunities we never
ght possible.

Start with finding just ONE
thing you can do differently
and better than anyone else.
Then build on that.

IDEAS PEOPLE & CASH

Whether it's organic or by acquisition, these are the three critical elements you need to grow any business.

1. IDEAS
It usually starts with an idea or innovation. The light-bulb moment, inspired by something we've experienced or noticed, when our mind is at its most relaxed and reflective, generally away from work. Large businesses brainstorm and hot-house to achieve breakthrough thinking, rarely having much to show for it. This is the weapon of the smaller, more nimble enterprise, who can be ideas rich but cash

poor. Separate the 'inventor' from the implementation as they're too emotionally involved and consider incubating the idea off-site to maintain momentum and avoid distraction.

2. PEOPLE

Once the idea has been sense checked, we need the right people to make it a reality. Ideas are easy – implementation is tough. Too often 'spare' people become the project team, chosen because they're not gainfully employed elsewhere. (That should tell you something). Instead, assemble a 'Go Team,' the very best people we have with a proven record of start-ups and making ideas work.

3. CASH

Most ideas need some capital to support their launch before they produce a return. Setting aside sufficient cash is usually where most ideas come unstuck, running out of budget before they have a chance to demonstrate their value. If the cash isn't available consider a joint venture or licensing the idea. Better to have a small part of a big idea, than no part at all.

It's very rare to simultaneously possess all three elements, but if we do, investors, banks and buyers will beat a path to our door.

THE TOP LINE

When times are
tough and we're
experiencing a downturn,
its common practice, but not
always common sense, that we
turn to cost-cutting and margin
reduction as the short-term solution.

The marketing budget, which underpins the sales
effort, and preserves the top line, is often pruned
back to the basics, instead of ring-fencing it.

Certainly review all costs and take out any fat or
discretionary spend that isn't justified. But we can't
continue to do this or there will be no business left.

Switch your focus to how the top line, revenue, can be
maintained.

▶ Is the marketing plan fit for purpose, given the prevailing market conditions?

▶ Should we re-allocate spend to increase the marketing budget?

▶ Are the sales team up to the task?

▶ Do they need additional support and resource?

▶ Can non-sales people help in any way?

▶ Are we close enough to our key customers? This is a time to really build relationships.

▶ Are all of our staff adequately briefed and 'on message'? They are our best brand ambassadors.

Reducing your revenue expectations, as is often the case, sets us up to fail and makes it acceptable to preside over a reducing top line. Stick with your revenue budget and focus all your attention on how this can be achieved.

WRITE IT RIGHT

This may seem trivial but it's actually quite important.

If we want things to happen as we want, write our own minutes and action points, don't give this task to our p.a. or anyone else.

Make notes in the moment.

Type these up within 24 hours whilst our memory is fresh.

If, on reflection, something important was overlooked, highlight this point, denoting it's an afterthought but should still be noted or actioned.

Write it right and it will happen......... right.

Write e-mails with care as ease and speed can make us sloppy. Call me old fashioned, but proper punctuation and grammar is more professional than composing it like a text message.

THE BURNING PLATFORM

If we want to bring about dramatic change we are wasting our time without a........ **Burning Platform**

Most of us distrust change. It makes us feel insecure, suspicious, and destabilised. Being outside our comfort zone is something we like to say but don't often practice.

We only buy into change, really commit to it, if our security is being threatened, individually or collectively.

A big set-back, such as losing a major customer or an aggressive new competitor arriving on the scene, are wake up calls to get our act together. To embrace change.

If we feel comfortable and satisfied, we can't see the need for change.

A burning platform, hot and dangerous, a state of emergency, means to survive we have to..........**Jump!**

Don't waste a good crisis.

A FEW GREAT PEOPLE ..

...make one great business.

Whether we are running an immense organisation, or a very small one, the top team rule applies. Look around the board room table at the people entrusted with making our company great, and ask this question.

Are we making do with mediocrity? And why? Possibly because we're afraid that...

..they've been here a long time and the thought of replacing them is in a box marked 'don't open.'

..they have equity and we'd have to buy them out.

..their performance might improve - they were great once.

..they know where the dead bodies are buried.

..how would it look to staff and customers?

Our top team enables us to keep a clear desk whilst looking at the horizon. If we're having to tackle too much every day detail, either we're a poor delegator, or we're compensating for some poor performers in our top team.

Get the team right and the sky's the limit.

Keep them match fit and you will keep on winning.

"If you want to travel fast, go alone. If you want to travel far, go together."

WHAT ARE WE DOING RIGHT?

It's human nature that we learn very little when we're on a roll and things are going well. When the chips are down, we discuss, debate, analyse our way out of a crisis, hoping we remember this stuff next time round.

We are scarred by bad times and remember.

We take good times for granted and forget.

Remember when we were on a roll and things were going right. Wouldn't it be invaluable to recall what we were doing then that led to that run of good fortune?

If we are sustaining high performance, record our magic ingredients, our formula, so that we know how to repeat this, again and again.

When there are changes of management, some of our best ideas are rejected and lost, replaced by fresh techniques introduced in order for new egos to stamp their identity.

Do we find ourselves wondering ..

Why did we stop doing that?
It always seemed to work!

Consider capturing your magic formula as a mathematical equation. For example:
CM + AS = HM%
Creative Marketing + Awesome Service = High Margin

DON'T LET THE DETAIL ..

.. destroy the deal.

Deals are done because two parties trust each other and believe they can create value by working together or conducting a transaction.

The honeymoon period includes identifying the initial opportunity and target, the seduction early in the relationship, the bristle of excitement when we feel something worthwhile may transpire. All this effort culminates in a short breath of celebration when we have reached in-principle agreement.

A Letter of Intent, Heads of Terms or Memorandum of Understanding is concluded, and everyone is feeling very pleased with themselves. Then we instruct lawyers.

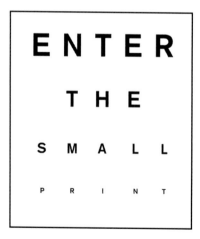

All the trust that has been garnered along the way is gradually dissipated. So many questions you hadn't thought of, so much downside if things don't pan out the way you expected. So much time to complete the transaction you hardly remember why you wanted to do it in the first place.

With any deal there are key elements that make it work for both parties. Focus on getting these right and don't allow ourselves to be hijacked by the rest.

Many deals are aborted at an advanced stage, when we have invested a great deal of energy and money, often falling down on a comparatively small detail. Both parties, led by their lawyers concerned to protect us, dig in on a point of principle, and trust, and can't find a way back.

A great opportunity missed because we allowed the detail to destroy the deal.

SHUT UP

Children used to be told they should be seen and not heard.

The most verbose person in a meeting isn't necessarily the most senior, or smart, they just like the sound of their own voice. They crave air time.

Sometimes, the most senior (and smart) person will say virtually nothing, then ask the killer question just as the meeting is coming to a close. This makes a huge impact.

It's quite a good habit **never to speak first.**

Wait until we've assessed the situation.

Work out the **power** dynamics in the room.

Closely **observe** body language.

Listen for clues for which buttons to press.

Then replay their argument in our own words.

They're astounded by our intuition and we connect.

In a lengthy and important negotiation, we often reach
a critical point where we either walk away or resolve it.

The moment of truth.

That's when silence can prove truly powerful.
Who will blink first?
Maintain radio silence and let them, not us, break it.
When they break cover, we know we have got them.

MAKING A CRISIS LESS OF A DRAMA

At some point in our careers turbulence turns to crisis and that is when our leadership skills are truly tested. Here are some thoughts to help navigate the stormy period:

- **Tone & Pace** need to be adapted to suit the situation

- **Morale & Mood** are boosted in direct proportion to honesty

- **Be Visible**, don't hide

- **Project** calm, considered confidence, but not courage

- **Keep a Log** for the next time this happens

- **Use Humour** to break the tension but with care and in context

- Create a **War Cabinet** in extreme circumstances

- Assess the **Worst Case Scenario** – is this a bump or a crater?

- Have a **Road Map** but be ready to course correct

- **Communicate** in bite sized chunks as too much might spook the horses

- Stay true to your **Business Model** as it's not necessarily broken

Stay true to your **Values** as this is when they really count

Choose the **Best Man** for the job as it might not be you

PREP OR IMPROV

Stand-up comedians love the challenge of improvisation but few can pull it off. When it works it's mesmerising but even the most talented give in to the safety of preparation and rehearsal.

As we hone our skills and our confidence grows, we can become lazy at preparation and opt instead for the high wire adrenalin rush of spontaneity. We like winging it, responding off the cuff, using our wits and our senses. Spontaneous action is fun.

The more linear thinkers will adopt preparation as their default and stick to the script. This can appear stiff and inflexible and cannot adequately legislate for the curve ball we sometimes like to throw. We're caught off guard and don't have the ability to improvise. What is the right balance between these two approaches?

Consider ...
1. What impression do we want to create?
How do we want to be perceived and play to this.
2. What outcome do we want to achieve?
Ensure we know why we're there and what we want to get out of it. It's so frustrating to hit the street afterwards and think "Why oh why did we forget to say that??"

If we are clear on these, then our preparation is complete and we can be as spontaneous as we like. Provided we keep this front of mind throughout we will come away having made the right impression and ready to move forward.

START-UPS...

..are not for the faint hearted, but are enormously rewarding, both personally and commercially, if they work. Four out of five start-ups in the UK fail, usually because they run out of money. If you've never been part of a start-up, do one – it's a wonderfully exhilarating roller-coaster ride with the steepest learning curve you'll ever climb. Here are some ground rules:

Do The Research Yourself – with potential customers – so you can hear their comments first hand and warm them up to the idea of buying from us later. Then sense check to get an objective view from smart people who are unconnected with the project.

Just Because It's Never Been Done doesn't mean it won't work. Previous cracks at it may have failed because the timing or execution were poor.

Find An Obsessive Leader – who has absolute belief and commitment, no concept of failure, is prepared to lobby, cajole, break the rules, stick their neck on the line, in order to succeed.

Ignorance Can Be Better Than Experience – if we know how big the hill is going to be, we won't climb it. Some of the most magnificent start-ups are by people who had no clue about how tough the venture might be. Ignorance also enables us to bring fresh thinking without the baggage of the past.

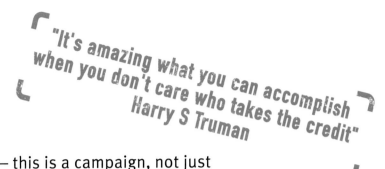
"It's amazing what you can accomplish when you don't care who takes the credit"
Harry S Truman

Campaign Team – this is a campaign, not just another project. Choose your team accordingly, remembering that the idea is the easy bit, making it happen if really tough. A good idea will fail with a poor team, but an average idea can succeed with a first rate one.

Brand It – giving the project a dramatic name is motivational and makes it real.

Captain Objective – to act as a foil to the Obsessive Leader, appoint someone divorced from the project to ask the difficult questions and keep us from falling off a cliff. They monitor progress against our milestones and control speculative costs.

Time Lag – is inevitable. It always takes twice as long as you reckoned.

Budget Reality – the costs must include a healthy contingency because we're venturing into the unknown, and the revenue will fall far short of our expectations, because of optimistic naivety. As a consequence, be prepared to inject a further round of funding and further rounds after that.

Failure Impact – assess the damage to our finances and confidence that an aborted project may cause. Ensure the campaign team know that their jobs are safe and they have somewhere to return to if we abort; this will take the pressure off them and they will perform even better.

STOP DOING, START THINKING

Turn off your computer and phones.
Sit back.
Relax.
Focus on your breathing.
Empty your head.
Stay empty headed.
Now allow yourself to reflect on what's important
today.

Look out of the window or at something that pleases
you.
Ignore the weird glances from your colleagues.
If this isn't working leave the office, find somewhere
quiet and start again.

We all need time to stop and stare but sadly this
behaviour is prone to ridicule.
If we're spotted reflecting we'll probably say we're
having a migraine.
We're not likely to say: "It's OK. I'm just thinking.."
although this is the truth.

And what's wrong with that?

Our brains need a rest, especially when they have
been intensely active.
Our greatest breakthroughs come when we are in this
reflective state.
We rarely solve a problem when our mind is
overheated.

In the Far East contemplation rooms, where we are
free to sit and think, are quite common. This is viewed
with respect as it creates wisdom and perspective.

Can't we all find time to do a bit more of that?

A GOAL SETTING PROCESS

1. **Find A Quiet Place** – give yourself the time and space, without distraction, to be reflective and relaxed in considering your goals.

2. **Engage Both Head & Heart** – capture all the things you want to BE, DO & HAVE. For example, "I want to BE more fulfilled; I want to advance my career; I want to HAVE a new home." Against each goal, say why this is really important to you, and also consider the consequence of not achieving the goal.

3. **Decide What's Important** and ask yourself "WHAT'S MISSING IN MY LIFE?" – for example: family; friendships; relationships; partner; career; financial; physical well-being; emotional well-being. Rank these in order of importance.

4. **Set A Time Horizon** – divide your goals into four groups:
• On-going goals needing daily attention
• Short term goals to achieve within a month or so
• Medium term goals which will take up to a year to achieve
• Long term goals that will take much longer than a year

5. **What Will I Need To Get There?** Consider the support and resources you will require to achieve your goals and who you might share this with to keep you on track.

6. **Think 'Smarter'** – ensure your goals are: Specific, Motivational, Attainable, Relevant, Trackable, Enjoyable, Rewarding. You need to stretch yourself whilst being realistic - within your power and control to achieve. Also, don't handicap your chances of success by having too many goals – you should be able to recall your goals without referring to a list.

7. **Personal + Corporate** – these need to compliment, not conflict, so that work/life balance is in harmony. (For example, a goal to be more hands-on with the Far East office might well clash with a goal to have more quality time with your family)

8. **Do The Rocking Chair Test** – now sit back and notice how these goals feel, visualise yourself achieving what you have set down, amending if the goals you have set don't feel right or don't excite you.

 **Now get on with it**..

CORPORATE HEALTH CHECK

Depending on our age we may have a health screening with our consultant every couple of years. This measures our level of health against the previous year's tests and triggers remedial action. It's good practice to also do this with our company, but using a rather different set of tests, scoring yourself from (1) = poor to (10) = outstanding:

People
- ☐ CEO > Leadership Effectiveness
- ☐ Senior Management Team > Calibre
- ☐ Succession Planning > Key People
- ☐ Organisation Structure > Fit For Purpose
- ☐ Alignment > Management & Shareholders
- ☐ Culture & Values > Commitment
- ☐ Talent Management > Recruiting & Inducting
- ☐ Internal Communications
- ☐ Management Capacity > Growth Potential
- ☐ Creativity & Innovation > Spirit Of Enterprise

Customers
- ☐ Customer Retention %
- ☐ Dominant Customer %
- ☐ New Customer Acquisition
- ☐ Order Fulfilment Consistency
- ☐ Customer Service Standards

Business Development
- ☐   Strategy & Vision - Progress
- ☐   Brand Identity & Awareness
- ☐   Product/Market Development
- ☐   Market Share %
- ☐   Market Intelligence

Governance & Infrastructure
- ☐   IT Systems & Technology
- ☐   Controls & Processes
- ☐   Risk Management
- ☐   Property & Facilities
- ☐   Procurement Efficiency

Cash & Capital
- ☐   Financial Controls
- ☐   Accuracy Of Forecasting
- ☐   Year On Year Profit Growth %
- ☐   Achievement Of Target Margin %
- ☐   Cash flow & Funding Headroom
- ☐   Enterprise Value (Compared To Previous Year)

Commitments & Deadlines

We commit to the following actions to improve our corporate health...

ENCORE ANXIETY

As we become more and more successful we expect our appetite for risk to increase. It doesn't, for two main reasons

1. Because our reputation becomes all important, and
2. If we have built personal wealth we are concerned about losing it

In spite of this we remain plagued by the need to repeat our greatest triumphs, feeding our ego and savouring that adrenalin kick once again. Our need to prove to ourselves we're still the big hitter we once were and can do it again.

We have built an able executive team and discover that with a clearer desk comes less fulfilment, because we appear to be doing less in the business and we miss the coal face, doing deals and making things happen.

The business is mature and stable, but this steady state does not suit our temperament.

We have a dangerous
condition. We are suffering
from...**Encore Anxiety.**

Someone with this
condition can be pretty
irresponsible.

Changing things for
change sake.
Doing deals because
they're a deal junkie.
Coming up with crazy ideas
that will revolutionise our
world.
Creating instability
because we need to prove
we're still valued.

How do you cure Encore
Anxiety?

I wish I knew. Sadly, I am a
chronic case.

RISKY BUSINESS

Our attitude to risk is often the most divisive issue in the board room.

The pleasure derived from the potential gain is never as great as the pain from the potential loss.

The fear of failure, of damage to reputation and wealth, freezes us into a state where we cannot move forward for fear of going backward.

But unless we are growing we are shrinking, both as individuals and corporations.

So how can we overcome these demons, balancing attitude with altitude?

Scenario plan. Visualise and map out the downside. Is it really so scary?
Remove judgement. If we separate the perception of others we will be less afraid of risk.
Choose language. Replace 'fear of failure' with 'fear of not succeeding.'
Training experience. We cannot fail, we can only learn.
Confidence conquers. Risk is a state of mind. There is no certainty in life. If you want it enough it will happen.

REBEL WITH A CAUSE

Whilst we all recognise the importance of team and the dangers of the 'wunderkind' every business, from time to time, needs at least one rebel to shake it up, challenge behaviour and change course.

This might be the leader but more likely will be someone lower down the hierarchy who is passionate and obstinate and prepared to break the rules to get things done.

They have a kind of Triple 'A' status, seeking out...

Ambition   Adventure   Achievement

Like the sheriff in the western, they ride into town, kill the bad guys, set new values and beliefs, and ride off into the sunset.

They don't stay for long, but leave their mark.

Don't be afraid of these people.

They are not 'terrorists' they are 'missionaries.'

They can change our world.

SELL TOO EARLY

Much is written about the art of the exit. When asked how he became so rich, John Paul Getty replied:

"BY SELLING TOO EARLY"

Selling, and of course, buying, is all about timing. We need to read the cycle, of our sector, the economy, and the financial world, from both a debt and equity perspective. If these are in alignment, and confidence is high, we may sell more easily and at a full price.

But also take into account that selling a business is a very lengthy process and by the time we are ready to complete, the market may have cooled, as well as the buyer.

So, if we're intent on an exit, and the price meets expectations, don't be persuaded to wait till the market ripens.

Don't be greedy.

Sell too early.

Enjoy the cash and move on with the next phase of life.

HIGH TIME FOR A 'CSO'

Selling is the lifeblood of any healthy business yet we still tend to treat sales people with some contempt. Perhaps their outwardly aggressive and confident character makes them unattractive and loses friends in the workplace, but this masks a bigger issue.

Given that nothing actually happens until something is sold, isn't it surprising that we have Chiefs of just about everything, except Sales.

We have Commercial Directors but they also aren't Chiefs and this role usually carries wider responsibilities than the sales function.

Why not be the first company around to create an important new title?

Sales people should be proud of the critical part they play in commerce but also learn that a little bit of humility will help their cause in earning more respect in and around the business, finding their rightful place alongside the other Chiefs.

CHIEF

Sales
Officer

Acknowledgements

I've met a great many interesting and successful people over the years and made it my business to learn from each of them. My Dad, Sam, was my first mentor but not in a traditional sense, mostly using bollockings to make his point. He taught me about conviction and compassion in equal measure.

I have tried to recollect those who have influenced my thinking or lent me their ideas whilst writing this. Tim Pilcher for making numbers simple; Chris Hughes on being funny; Adrian Spink for post-it values and CSO thinking; Alastair Kight for the sleep-over test; Caspar Berry and Jack Morris on risk; Jennifer Holloway on the handshake moment; Darren Rudkin on sword and shield and check-in; Rosie Walford on goal setting; Vince Tickel for simply loads of great advice.

Thanks to Des Wilson for his editing advice and occasional patience, Otto Dettmer for his unique illustrations, and Jeremy Thompson at Matador Publishing who made the process as painless as possible.

Finally, to my wife and valued critic, Jennifer, who read the early drafts before anyone, in a bar in Ibiza, giving me the confidence to carry on the project, with her customary common sense.

"LIFE IS NOT A JOURNEY TO THE GRAVE WITH THE GOAL OF ARRIVING SAFELY IN A PRETTILY PRESERVED BODY, BUT RATHER TO SKID IN SIDEWAYS IN A SHOWER OF GRAVEL AND PARTY SHARDS, THOROUGHLY EXHAUSTED, LOUDLY PROCLAIMING: FUCK ME – THAT WAS BRILLIANT!"

About the Author

Most careers start out with you working for someone else, aspiring to becoming your own boss at some point. Andrew Morris has done the very opposite.

After dropping out of college and a short stint in high-end fashion retail, he entered the family shop-fitting and property business. At 21 he was running a subsidiary selling fake fur coats to Scandinavia, had a short shock in electro-plating in Nottingham, and then returned to the core business in a sales and marketing role.

He launched father Sam's Business Design Centre in Islington and, after getting a taste for exhibitions and media, went on to run Earls Court & Olympia, majority owned by Candover, and the National Exhibition Centre, wholly owned by Birmingham City Council.

Starting a portfolio career in 2007 he went full circle, back to owning and running a niche business, the Academy for Chief Executives, which aims to be the No 1 organisation for CEOs wishing to be No 1.

His mantra is "take your job seriously, but not yourself."

BUSINESS TO GO

simple ideas to takeaway

Andrew B Morris

This book is designed for today's time-poor, over-loaded entrepreneurs, who will find this pragmatic, no-nonsense approach an invaluable take-away. Original ideas drawn from experience, rather than business school - stuff that really works – and, importantly, can be easily implemented.

Building a successful business is about keeping it simple, working out what works, and minimising unforced errors. This takes time to perfect but reading this will help get you there faster, providing a broad range of practical ideas drawn from over 30 years of personal leadership experience.

Business To Go will stimulate your thinking when you're stuck, or just need re-assurance that you're making the right call. Written in a direct and concise style, with quirky typography and illustrations, it will appeal to ambitious executives with big plans who don't have cash to throw around.